On the Tracks of Dinosaurs

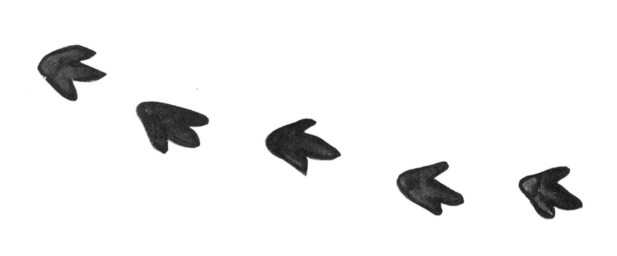

On the Tracks of Dinosaurs

BY
James O. Farlow, Ph.D.

ILLUSTRATIONS BY
Doris Tischler

Franklin Watts

New York | London | Toronto | Sydney | 1991

For Eric and Jill, as well as Chrystal, Brian, Jason, and any future nieces or nephews

Most photographs were taken by the author
Some photographs courtesy of Philip F. Currie, Eric R. Piarka, and James E. Whitcraft

Library of Congress Cataloging-in-Publication Data

Farlow, James Orville.
   On the tracks of dinosaurs / by James O. Farlow : illustrations by Doris Tischler.
        p.   cm.
   Includes bibliographical references and index.
   Summary: Describes the formation and discovery of fossilized dinosaur footprints and how paleontologists use them to learn about the probable nature and behavior of the animals who made them.
   ISBN 0-531-15220-0—ISBN 0-531-10991-7 (lib. bdg.)
   1. Footprints. Fossil—Juvenile literature.   2. Dinosaurs—Juvenile literature. [1. Footprints, Fossil.   2. Dinosaurs.
3. Fossils.   4. Paleontology.] I. Tischler, Doris, ill.
II. Title.
QE845.F37   1991
567.9'1—dc20   90-19432 CIP AC

Contents

CHAPTER ONE

The Discovery of Dinosaur Footprints

We all enjoy monster movies about dinosaurs and other huge prehistoric creatures. Godzilla, Gorgo, Gwangi, and the Beast from 20,000 Fathoms chew up buildings and stomp on tanks, and we cheer them on. Have you ever wondered, though, what *real* dinosaurs were like as living animals? How did they walk and run? Did dinosaurs live by themselves, or did they live in groups? And how can we know today what living dinosaurs were like so long ago?

Nobody has ever seen a living dinosaur, and yet **paleontologists** (scientists who study fossils) know that these great reptiles once lived on our planet. Fossilized bones of dinosaurs have been found on every continent.

Bones and skeletons are not the only fossils of dinosaurs that we have, however. Fossils also include the footprints of dinosaurs that occur in rocks around the world. In some places, these fossil tracks are very common.

In this book, we will look at how dinosaur footprints became fossils. We will also see how paleontologists study dinosaur tracks and use them to learn things that would be hard to discover from bones alone: things about the way dinosaurs walked and ran and how they acted as living creatures.

Early Jurassic three-toed tracks of bipedal dinosaurs from northern Arizona

Emus at the San Diego Zoo

When dinosaur footprints were first discovered, pale-ontologists did not yet know enough about dinosaurs to realize that they had made the tracks. In the year 1802, when the United States was a very young country, people began to find strange footprints in the rocks of the Connecticut River valley in the states of Massachusetts and Connecticut. Some of these three-toed, birdlike footprints were as much as half a meter (about 20 inches) long.

Scientists who studied the tracks decided that these fossil footprints had been made by big **flightless birds** (birds that cannot fly), like the Australian emu (a bird about

8

When dinosaur footprints were first discovered, scientists thought that they had been made by large, extinct, flightless birds.

as tall as a person), the African ostrich, the South American rhea, and the cassowary of New Guinea. Explorers on the islands of New Zealand had recently found the bones of **extinct** birds called moas, which were even bigger than the biggest living flightless birds. Huge birds like moas must have lived in prehistoric New England, the scientists decided.

The rocks in which the Connecticut River valley footprints were found formed during the time of the dinosaurs. In the early 1800s, however, complete dinosaur skeletons had not yet been found. No one knew that some kinds of dinosaurs had walked on hind legs that ended in three-toed, birdlike feet. Beginning in the middle of the 1800s, though, very well-preserved dinosaur skeletons began to be discovered, including skeletons of the two-legged kind with birdlike feet. Paleontologists at last realized that the remarkable "birds" of ancient New England had in fact been dinosaurs.

CHAPTER TWO

Introducing the Dinosaurs

Before we can say much about dinosaur footprints, we need to know something about the animals that made them and the time when those trackmakers lived. **Geologists** (scientists who study the earth and its history) divide the history of the earth into large amounts of time called **periods**. Each period lasted millions of years. Several periods are grouped together into even larger amounts of time called **eras**.

Eras and periods of earth history. Dinosaurs lived during the Triassic, Jurassic, and Cretaceous periods of the Mesozoic Era.

Era	Period	Millions of Years Before Present	
CENOZOIC	Quaternary	2	First Humans
	Neogene	24	Modern Mammal Groups Common
	Paleogene	66	First Large Mammals
MESOZOIC	Cretaceous	144	Last Dinosaurs
	Jurassic	208	First Birds
	Triassic	245	First Dinosaurs and Mammals
PALEOZOIC	Permian	286	
	Pennsylvanian	320	
	Mississippian	360	First Reptiles
	Devonian	408	First Amphibians
	Silurian	438	
	Ordovician	505	Early Fishes
	Cambrian	570	Animals with Shells Common
PRECAMBRIAN		3900	First Living Things

11

Late Triassic animals from northern Arizona. Three small meat-eating dinosaurs (*Coelophysis*) eat a dead aetosaur. Attracted to the kill are three other meat-eaters: In the water swims a crocodile-like phytosaur, and above it a small, long-legged, true crocodile moves cautiously along the water's edge; from beyond the crocodile comes one of the biggest meat-eaters of the Triassic Period, a rauisuchian. A metoposaur, a kind of water-living amphibian, nervously crawls away from the meat-eating reptiles. Of all these animals, only *Coelophysis* is a dinosaur.

A parade of dinosaurs, drawn to the same scale. From left to right: *Allosaurus*, *Brachiosaurus*, *Diplodocus*, *Apatosaurus*, *Stegosaurus*, *Iguanodon*, *Tyrannosaurus*, *Euoplocephalus*, *Anatotitan*, and *Triceratops*. The children on bicycles provide the scale.

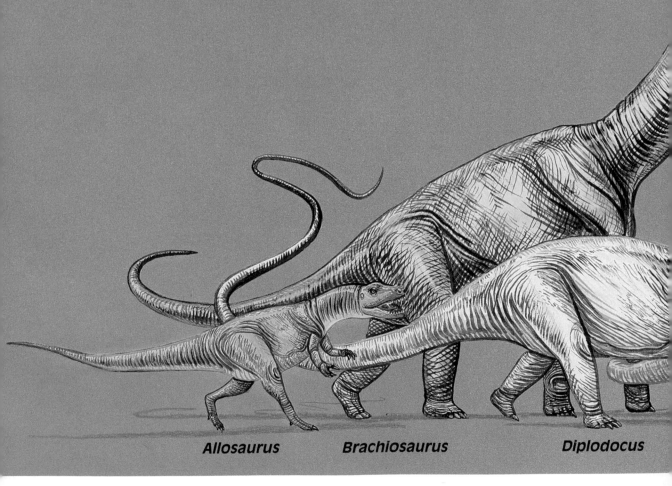

Allosaurus   *Brachiosaurus*   *Diplodocus*

Apatosaurus

Stegosaurus

15

Iguanodon

Tyrannosaurus

Euoplocephalus   *Anatotitan*   *Triceratops*

Bones of early dinosaurs are found in rocks that formed in the middle of the Triassic Period of the Mesozoic Era, about 230 million years ago. Footprints that may have been made by the first dinosaurs occur in rocks a little older than that. Early dinosaurs were not very big. They lived in a world filled with other, often larger, reptiles. Footprints of these other reptiles are usually more common than those of dinosaurs in rocks older than the late part of the Triassic Period.

By the end of the Triassic Period, nearly all of the other big reptiles were extinct. Dinosaurs had become the most important group of large land animals. Many kinds of large and small dinosaurs lived in the Jurassic and Cretaceous periods, which followed the Triassic. The last dinosaurs became extinct at the end of the Cretaceous Period (which was also the end of the Mesozoic Era), about 65 million years ago.

Saurischian dinosaurs had hip skeletons similar to those of many other reptiles. **Theropods** were **bipedal** (two-legged) saurischian dinosaurs, and most of them were **carnivores** (meat eaters). Some theropods, like *Allosaurus* and *Tyrannosaurus*, were as big or bigger than elephants, but other theropods were only the size of chickens. **Sauropods** were **quadrupedal** (four-legged), long-necked **herbivores** (plant eaters), and were also the biggest dinosaurs. *Apatosaurus* (once called *Brontosaurus*), *Diplodocus*, and *Brachiosaurus* are familiar sauropods.

Ornithischian dinosaurs had hip skeletons somewhat like those of birds, even though birds are probably more closely related to saurischians. All of the ornithischians were herbivores. Many ornithischians (like *Triceratops*, *Euoplocephalus*, and *Stegosaurus*) were quadrupedal animals. **Ornithopods** were large and small ornithischian dinosaurs, like *Iguanodon* and *Anatotitan*, that walked part of the time on four legs and part of the time on two.

The bones of different kinds of dinosaurs are not equally common, but skeletons of both bipedal and quadrupedal dinosaurs are often found. Fossilized dinosaur footprints are also found in many places, but although the tracks of bipedal dinosaurs like theropods and ornithopods are very common, footprints of quadrupedal dinosaurs are rare.

CHAPTER THREE

How Footprints Become Fossils

If you walk at the water's edge along a lake or the ocean, you leave a trail of footprints in the sand behind you. By the next day, however, your footprints will likely be gone, having been washed away by the waves. The same was true of footprints made by ancient animals like dinosaurs. The chances that any single footprint will become a fossil are very poor.

Fortunately for paleontologists, the chances that some footprints will become fossils improve when large numbers of footprints are being made. An animal takes many steps during its lifetime, and there are millions of track-making animals living at any one time. As a result, animals make so many footprints that it becomes more likely that some of the tracks will become fossils.

In order to make footprints, a dinosaur had to walk across soft sediments. **Sediments** are loose pieces of material that pile up on the earth's surface. Some sediments form by the **weathering** and **erosion** of rocks. Other sediments form by chemical reactions that occur in water. Still other sediments are made when animals, plants, or tiny ocean creatures make shells or other hard parts using the **mineral** calcium carbonate (lime).

Geologists name sediments by the size of the materials in them. Boulders, cobbles, and gravel are large sediment pieces. Sands are much smaller materials. Smaller still are muds called silts, and even tinier are the very fine muds called clays.

Over time, layers of sediment become sedimentary rocks. Sediment pieces become pressed or cemented together, or the mineral crystals that originally made up the sediment take a new form. Sometimes these changes occur quickly, but sometimes they happen very slowly. The change from sediments to sedimentary rocks can take place either at the earth's surface or at the bottom of thickly piled sediment layers. Sands become sandstones, silts and clays become siltstones and shales, and lime sediments become limestones or, under some conditions, dolomites.

Most footprints that finally become fossils are made when animals cross new layers of sediment deposited along the edges of rivers, lakes, or seas during storms or floods. The first such sediments to be laid down are often sands. As the waters that carried the sediment become calmer, particles of clay settle to the bottom. This makes a thin, muddy surface above the sand. This surface is perfect for recording tracks once the water becomes shallow or drains away. After the next flood or storm, a new layer of sand will bury the clay layer. When all of these sediments become rock, the clay layer may become a weak spot in

When a dinosaur walked across a sediment surface, its weight sometimes bent sediment layers below the one on which the dinosaur walked (top drawing). If these layers could be separated, as shown in the middle group of drawings, we would see ghost tracks below the real footprint. Footprints can be preserved either as natural molds (brown layer in bottom two drawings) or natural casts (yellow layer).

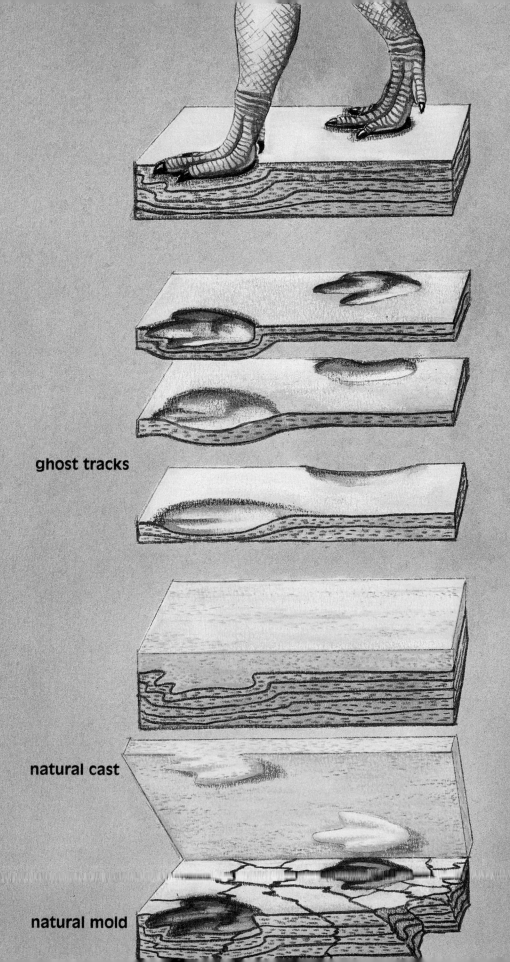

ghost tracks

natural cast

natural mold

the rock. Because of this, the sandstone above the clay layer may easily separate from the sandstone below it, exposing any footprints that were made in the clay surface.

Often, however, a footprint is filled by sediments that are different from those in which the animal walked. Such different sediments will become sedimentary rocks that differ in properties that affect their resistance to erosion. If the rock layers containing the footprint are uncovered by erosion, the different strengths of the two sedimentary rocks will cause the weaker rock to be eroded first. Then

Scale impressions of an Early Jurassic theropod dinosaur footprint from New England

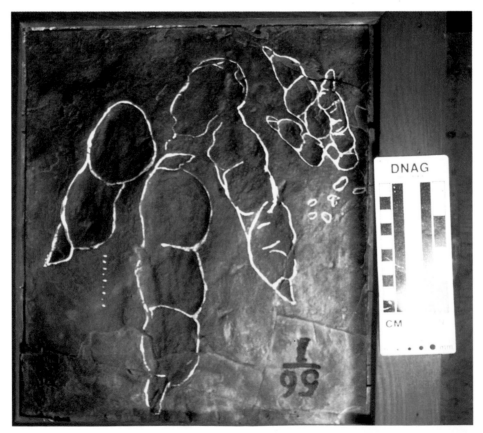

24

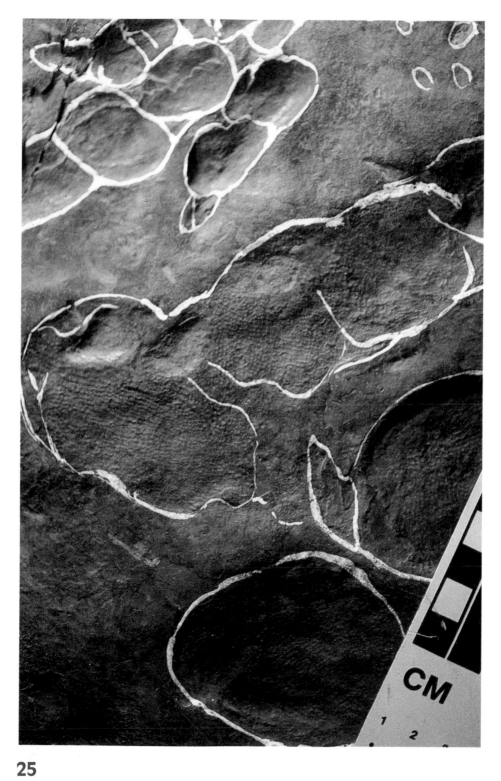

25

the footprint will again be visible after millions of years of burial.

Suppose that the sediment in which the trackmaker walked becomes the more resistant rock. The newly uncovered footprint will then be a depression in the upper surface of this rock— a **natural mold**. Suppose instead that the sediment that filled the track becomes the more resistant material. In that case, the footprint will be exposed as rock sticking out from the bottom of the rock layer that covered the surface across which the dinosaur once moved. A footprint preserved this way is a **natural cast**.

As a dinosaur walked across a sediment layer, a footprint was made in that layer, as we have already seen. At the same time, though, layers of sediment beneath the one on which the dinosaur walked were also bent by the dinosaur's weight to form a series of footprints stacked one on top of the other. Such underlying footprints are called **ghost tracks**, or **undertracks**. Because the pressure from the dinosaur's foot became less and less in sediment layers further below the top layer, ghost tracks become less clear the further beneath the "real" footprint they are. The marks of the toes become fainter, until all that remains is an oval-shaped depression. Sometimes ghost tracks can also form above the surface on which the dinosaur walked, if layers of mud very gradually filled the footprint.

It is often very difficult to tell whether a fossil footprint is a "real" track or a ghost track. Some paleontologists think that most footprints that become fossils are really ghost tracks. If a footprint has a very clear outline, and also preserves impressions of the scales of the bottom of the foot that made it, we can be sure that it is a print that was made in sediment that actually touched the trackmaker's foot.

26

CHAPTER FOUR

How Footprints Are Studied

Fossil dinosaur footprints are often found in rocks in the beds of modern-day rivers. People sometimes think that the tracks were made by dinosaurs that crossed the rivers. The dinosaurs made their footprints long before the rivers existed, however. The reason fossil tracks are so often found in riverbeds is that erosion by rivers uncovers sedimentary rock layers containing the tracks. If you could somehow remove all of the rocks on top of the track-containing layer on either side of a river, you would probably find fossil footprints there as well.

When a paleontologist finds fossil footprints in the field, he or she carefully measures and photographs the tracks, measures the distance between footprints, and makes a map of the tracksite. If possible, the better or more interesting footprints will be taken to the laboratory for later study. Usually the original footprints themselves are not taken. It may be too much work to cut out the rock containing them, or the owner of the land may not want the tracks removed.

Instead, the paleontologist makes copies of the footprints. Plaster of paris can be used to cast a natural mold footprint if the track has no undercuts. Undercuts are places where toes or edges of the print stick ahead or sideways into the rock below the top of the track. The footprint is greased with oil, after which a mixture of plaster and

Dinosaur footprints are often found in rocks in the beds of rivers.

**The author measuring an Early
Cretaceous dinosaur footprint in a creek
bed in Kimble County, Texas**

water is poured into it. When the plaster hardens, it separates cleanly from the track. If the footprint has undercuts, however, plaster cannot be used. When plaster is hard, it is not flexible, and so the cast catches on the undercuts. Many people do not understand this, and sometimes ruin footprints by filling them with plaster that cannot be removed easily. Footprints with undercuts must be copied with rubber compounds or other flexible materials.

A cast is very useful in studying differences in depth of different parts of a footprint. This in turn helps paleon-

The author making a plaster cast of a
dinosaur footprint at the Kimble County,
Texas, dinosaur footprint site

31

tologists to determine how the dinosaur carried its weight on its feet as it walked. The deeper any place in a footprint, the more weight was supported by the part of the foot that made that place. Such information may prove helpful in reconstructing the skeleton of the foot that made the track. Any part of the foot that usually supported a lot of the dinosaur's weight often had very strong bones.

Reconstructing the skeleton of the foot that made a footprint is the best way of identifying the kind of animal

Computer-drawn picture of an Early Cretaceous theropod dinosaur footprint from the bed of the Paluxy River at Dinosaur Valley State Park, near Glen Rose, Texas. Because the computer made the picture from a cast, the picture is upside-down from the way the real footprint would look. The different colors show differences in depth of the track: brown is deepest and light blue is shallowest. The track is about 50 centimeters long.

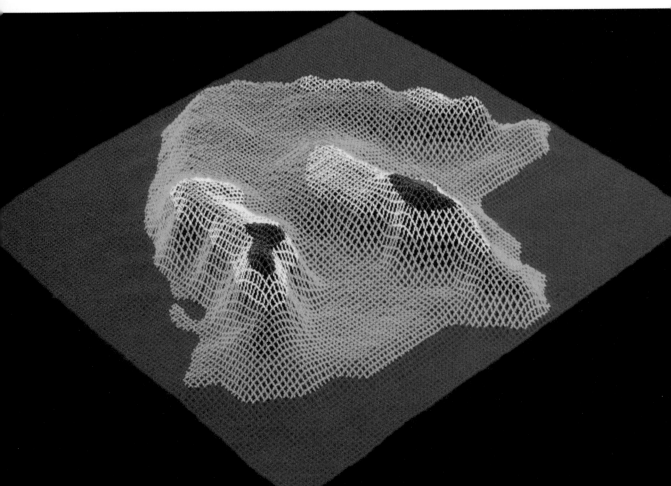

that made the print. Some well-preserved footprints have toe marks with clear swellings and narrow places. In lizards and most birds, swellings along the lengths of the toes usually mark the joints between individual toe bones. Paleontologists can similarly tell where the joints between toe bones in a dinosaur's foot were by looking at the position of swellings in the toe marks of the reptile's footprint. This in turn shows the length of the individual toe bones. A foot skeleton reconstructed from a footprint in this way can then be compared with actual foot skeletons of different dinosaurs in order to identify the dinosaur.

Unfortunately, toe pad swellings do not always match the joints between toe bones, and many dinosaur footprints do not have obvious toe pad swellings. Sometimes we can only guess at the maker of a footprint from the track's overall shape: Is the track longer than it is wide, or is it wider than long? Are the toes long and narrow, or short and wide? Do the toes end in sharp claw marks, or are they blunt? Are angles between toes large or small? All of these observations may help to identify the trackmaker, but they do not allow us to be as confident in our identification as we are when the foot skeleton can be reconstructed from toe pad swellings.

To make things even more difficult, the shape of a footprint can depend on many things besides the shape of the trackmaker's foot. The track may differ, for example, if the animal was running instead of walking, and speeding up instead of slowing down.

The sediment on which the dinosaur walked may also affect the appearance of its tracks. During the Jurassic Period, sauropod dinosaurs made footprints along the shore of a prehistoric lake in what is now southeastern Colorado. Some of these footprints are shallow and faint, and others deep, showing that the sediment across which the track-

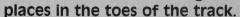

The foot skeleton of the dinosaur that made a footprint can sometimes be reconstructed from swellings and narrow places in the toes of the track.

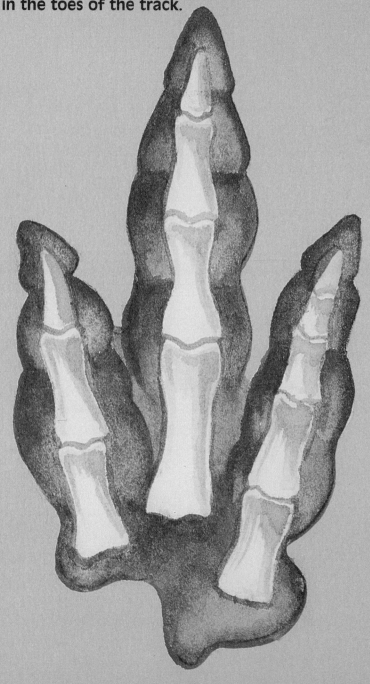

makers walked differed in its firmness. The deeper tracks were made in places under shallow water, and the shallow tracks were made in drier spots beyond the lake's edge.

We have already seen how ghost tracks formed in sediment layers below the layer on which the trackmaker moved can be very different from the "real" footprint in shape. A paleontologist might get the wrong idea about the kind of dinosaur that made a footprint when studying a ghost track that formed several layers below the layer on which the dinosaur actually walked.

The appearance of fossil footprints may even be affected by things that happen long after the tracks were made. If the rocks containing a footprint were squeezed and bent by movements of the earth's crust after the dinosaur lived, this may have greatly changed the shape of the footprint.

We can see that identifying the kind of dinosaur that made a footprint can be very difficult. Even if a paleontologist can say that a footprint was made by a theropod, for example, he or she can seldom be sure about which kind of meat-eating dinosaur made it. But suppose that paleontologists have found bones of a carnivorous dinosaur in the same area as where the theropod track was found, and in rocks of about the same age. If those bones show that the foot of the carnivore was the right size and shape to have made the footprint, then the paleontologist can decide that the footprint was probably made by the same type of dinosaur.

CHAPTER FIVE

How Footprints Are Named

If a paleontologist finds the bones of a new kind of dinosaur, he or she gives those remains a scientific name that other scientists can use in talking about the find. Scientific names have two parts, a generic name and a specific name. The generic name is like a person's last name, and the specific name is like his or her first name.

If the author wanted to write the names of his children like scientific names, they would be *Farlow jill* and *Farlow erin.* The generic name comes first and is always capitalized; the specific name is not capitalized. Both names are italicized or underlined.

Each species of dinosaur has its own generic and specific name, like *Apatosaurus louisae* and *Tyrannosaurus rex.* Some species of dinosaurs were very closely related, and so are given the same generic name, such as *Stegosaurus ungulatus* and *Stegosaurus stenops*—just as the author's two daughters, who are close relatives, have the same last name. When writing about how dinosaur species are related to each other, it is necessary to use both the generic and specific names, but in this book we will use only the generic names.

Dinosaur skeletons are examples of what paleontologists call **body fossils**—the preserved remains of long-dead animals. Fossil footprints, on the other hand, are traces of things that ancient creatures did while they were

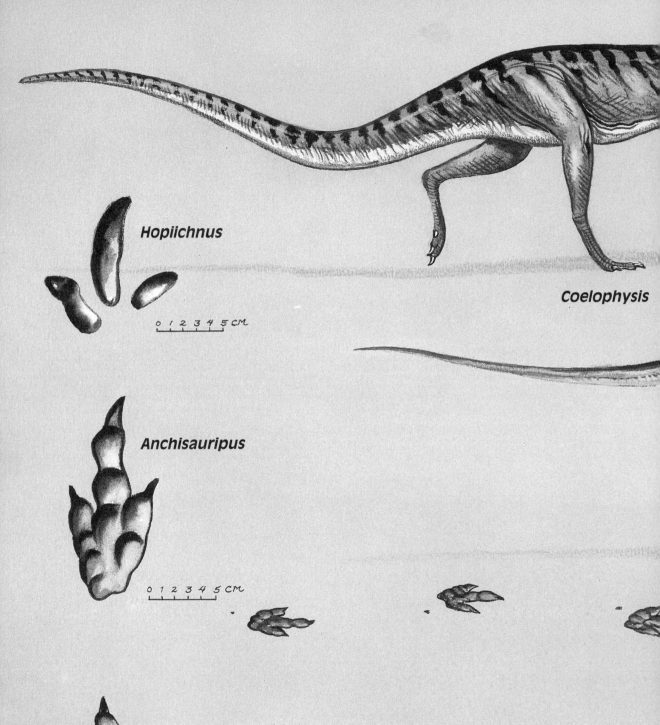

Hopiichnus

Coelophysis

0 1 2 3 4 5 CM

Anchisauripus

0 1 2 3 4 5 CM

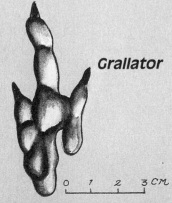

Grallator

0 1 2 3 CM

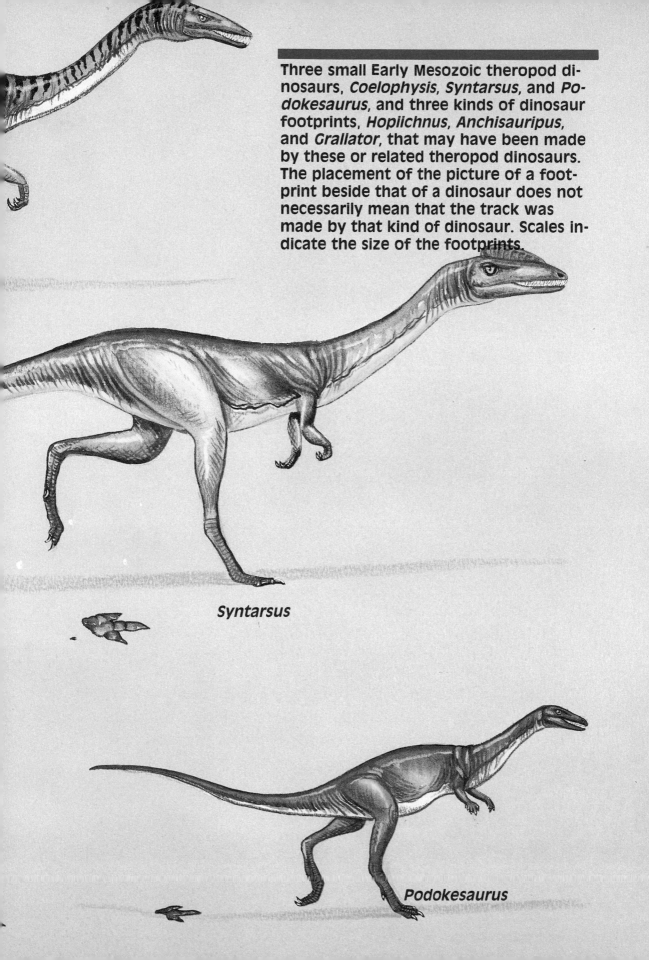

Three small Early Mesozoic theropod dinosaurs, *Coelophysis*, *Syntarsus*, and *Podokesaurus*, and three kinds of dinosaur footprints, *Hopiichnus*, *Anchisauripus*, and *Grallator*, that may have been made by these or related theropod dinosaurs. The placement of the picture of a footprint beside that of a dinosaur does not necessarily mean that the track was made by that kind of dinosaur. Scales indicate the size of the footprints.

Syntarsus

Podokesaurus

alive, and so are called **trace fossils**. Other trace fossils include burrows, nests, bite marks in bones or shells, and **coprolites** (fossilized droppings).

We can seldom be certain that we have correctly identified the makers of dinosaur footprints, and so paleontologists do not give the same scientific names to footprints that they give to skeletons. Bones of small theropods found in late Triassic and early Jurassic rocks of the southwestern United States were named *Coelophysis* and *Syntarsus*. A related dinosaur, *Podokesaurus*, is known from early Jurassic rocks of New England.

Three-toed footprints of small theropods occur in late Triassic and early Jurassic rocks of both New England and the Southwest. Some of these prints may have been made by *Coelophysis*, *Syntarsus*, or *Podokesaurus*, but many were probably made by other kinds of small theropods. Some may even be the footprints of babies of larger carnivorous dinosaurs. Consequently, the tracks have their own generic names, like *Hopiichnus*, *Grallator*, and *Anchisauripus*. Footprints are also given their own specific names.

Because it can be so hard to identify the makers of tracks, dinosaur footprints will probably never be as useful as dinosaur skeletons in comparing dinosaur **faunas** of different times and places. On the other hand, a dinosaur could die only once, and so could make only a single skeleton. When it was alive, though, it might have made huge numbers of footprints; any one dinosaur may have been more likely to leave a record of its presence as tracks than as bones. As a result, paleontologists may be more likely to find footprints than skeletons of dinosaurs that were rare when they were alive.

CHAPTER SIX

Walking and Running Dinosaurs

A human being walks with the entire length of the foot flat on the ground. Ground-living birds like emus and ostriches walk only on their toes, with their foot bones off the ground, acting like an added part of the leg.

Two-legged dinosaurs usually walked like birds do, with their foot bones well off the ground. Only their toe bones, and the parts of their foot bones that formed joints with the toe bones, touched the ground. This means that the rear of a bipedal dinosaur's footprint, what you might call a "heel," was usually made by the back of the toe region of the foot.

When you walk, your foot often does not point straight ahead. Instead, your left foot points a little to the left of the direction in which you are walking, and your right foot points a little to the right. We can say that your feet angle outward with respect to your direction of travel. Emus and ostriches also walk with their feet angled outward.

A sequence of footprints made by the same animal is called a **trackway** or **trail**. Most trackways of two-legged dinosaurs show that bipedal dinosaurs, unlike people, emus, and ostriches, walked with their toes turned a little inward, or "pigeon-toed." We can say that their feet angled inward with respect to their direction of travel.

The distance from a spot—like the tip of a toe—on one footprint in a trackway to the same spot on the next foot-

Feet of an emu, a theropod dinosaur, and a human being. Emus walk only on their toes, while people walk with their feet flat on the ground. Theropod dinosaurs, like emus, walked on their toes.

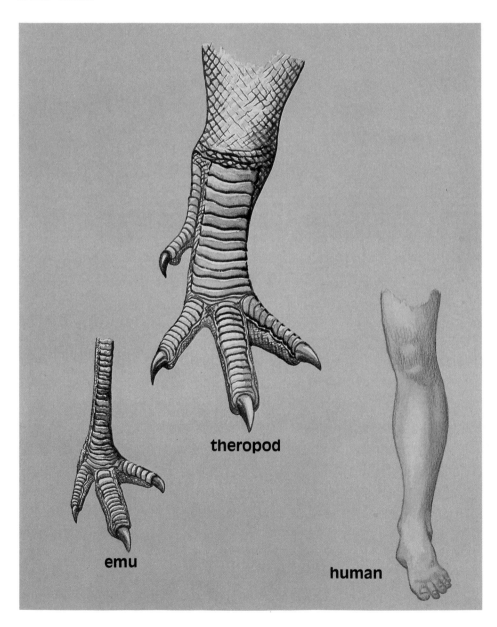

emu

theropod

human

42

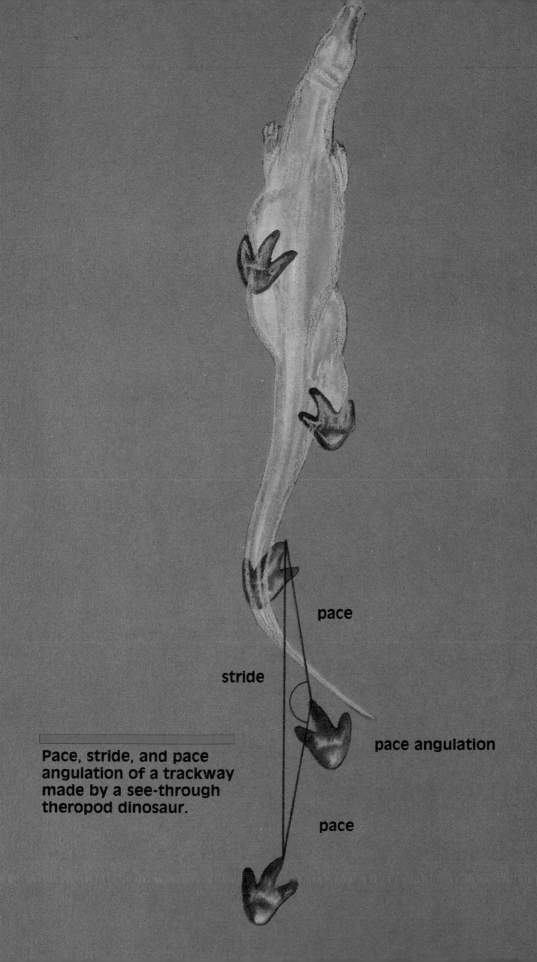

pace

stride

pace angulation

pace

Pace, stride, and pace angulation of a trackway made by a see-through theropod dinosaur.

print of the *opposite* side of the animal's body is called a **pace**. A pace could be, for example, the distance from the tip of the middle toe on a right footprint to the tip of the middle toe on the next left footprint, or the distance from the tip of the middle toe on a left footprint to the tip of the middle toe of the next right footprint.

The distance from a spot on one footprint to the same spot on the next footprint of the *same* side of the animal's body is a **stride**. Put another way, a stride is the distance from a right footprint to the next right print, or from one left track to the next.

One pace after another, and the stride made by the foot that touched the ground at the beginning and at the end of the two paces, make an imaginary triangle. The angle formed by the two paces is called the **pace angulation**.

If an animal walks by putting one foot directly in front of the other, the tracks made by the left and right feet will be in a single line. All of the animal's paces will be parts of this line, and every stride will be equal to the sum of two paces. Another way of describing this is to say that the pace angulation will be 180 degrees.

Usually, however, an animal does not place its feet one exactly in front of the other, and so the stride is less than the sum of the paces. The pace angulation is then less than 180 degrees.

In trackways made by most reptiles, the left and right

Trackway of a large monitor lizard in the desert of western Australia. The lizard put its hindfeet down on the ground close to footprints previously made by its forefeet. Unlike the trail of a bipedal dinosaur, the lizard's trackway is wide compared with the size of its footprints. Also, unlike most dinosaur trails, the lizard's trackway has a tail drag mark.

footprints are not in a single straight line but in two lines far apart from each other. The reptile's trackway is wide compared with the size of its footprints. The pace angulation of the trail is much less than 180 degrees.

The reason for this is that most reptiles walk with their upper "arm" and leg bones sticking straight out from their bodies; the bones of their lower "arms" and legs point downward from their elbows and knees. This makes a lizard look like it is trying to do push-ups as it walks.

The upper bone of the hindlimb of bipedal dinosaurs pointed nearly straight downward, or even a little inward. We would predict from this that a bipedal dinosaur placed its feet one almost in front of the other. Dinosaur trackways show that this prediction is correct. The trackway of a two-legged dinosaur is narrow compared with the size of its footprints; the pace angulation of a bipedal dinosaur's trail is much closer to 180 degrees than the pace angulation of a lizard trail is.

By walking with the hind legs directed straight downward, and by having long legs, bipedal dinosaurs were able to move their bodies farther forward in comparison with the length of each pace than is true of walking lizards. Walking with their legs directly beneath them also helped very large two-legged dinosaurs like *Tyrannosaurus* to support their immense weight better.

The stride of walking bipedal dinosaurs is usually about five to seven times the length of their footprints. A few trackways are known in which the stride is much longer compared with the size of the footprints. In Kimble County, Texas, for example, trackways of medium-size theropods were found in which the stride was fifteen to twenty times the length of the dinosaurs' tracks. These dinosaurs were probably running, perhaps at speeds of as much as 40 kilometers (almost 25 miles) per hour. At a site in Queensland,

46

Trackways prove that bipedal
dinosaurs, unlike lizards,
walked with their legs directly
beneath their bodies.

Trackway of a theropod dinosaur in the bed of the Paluxy River at Dinosaur Valley State Park, Glen Rose, Texas. The footprints are about 50 centimeters long.

Trackway of a running theropod dinosaur at the Kimble County, Texas, site. One footprint is just above the hammer, and the next is near the top of the picture. The footprints are about 37 centimeters long.

Australia, paleontologists found many trails of small and medium-size bipedal dinosaurs that may have been frightened into running by the approach of a big meat-eating dinosaur. In the western United States, very large footprints made by ornithopod dinosaurs sometimes occur in trails with very long paces, suggesting that their makers were running.

A few paleontologists believe that huge two-legged dinosaurs like *Tyrannosaurus* could run very rapidly. Other scientists doubt that, believing that these reptiles' legs were not strong enough for fast running. As yet, we have found no trackways made by very rapidly running theropods as big as *Tyrannosaurus*. This does not necessarily mean, though, that these gigantic carnivores did not run. *Tyrannosaurus* had such long legs that if it was capable of running rapidly, its paces might have been so long that many places where fossil footprints are found would not be big enough to include the footprints at both ends of such long steps. Furthermore, for so heavy an animal, a fall might have resulted in fatal injuries. Even if it could run, *Tyrannosaurus* may have done so only on dry, hard ground where the risk of slipping would not have been great. Unfortunately, footprints would have very little chance of being made and preserved in such places. We may never know for sure whether the biggest bipedal dinosaurs could run, and if so, at what speeds.

Old books and monster movies often show dinosaurs walking with their tails dragging on the ground. Dinosaur trackways hardly ever show marks made by dragging tails, however. Dinosaurs nearly always carried their tails well off the ground. For two-legged dinosaurs, the weight of the tail helped to balance the weight of the body over the dinosaur's hind legs.

Footprints of quadrupedal dinosaurs are much less common than those of bipeds. This is surprising, because skeletons of four-legged dinosaurs are often very common. Perhaps quadrupedal dinosaurs were less active than bipedal dinosaurs; maybe they took fewer steps and made fewer footprints. Another possibility is that four-legged dinosaurs did not visit the muddy places where footprints were likely to form and be preserved as often as two-legged dinosaurs did.

In comparison with the lengths of their legs, quadrupedal dinosaurs usually took shorter steps than bipedal dinosaurs. In most four-legged dinosaurs, the front legs were much shorter than the hind legs. If a quadrupedal dinosaur tried to take long steps, its short front legs might have had a hard time keeping up with its long hind legs, causing the dinosaur to trip over its own feet! Taking small steps may have made it easier for four-legged dinosaurs to keep their front and back legs working together properly.

Hindfoot tracks are much bigger than tracks of the forefeet. This shows that quadrupedal dinosaurs carried more weight on their back feet than on their front feet. Unlike bipedal dinosaurs, four-legged dinosaurs walked with their feet angling outward with respect to the direction of travel.

As a four-legged animal walks, the hindfoot on one side of its body starts to move forward while the forefoot on the same side of its body is still on the ground. By the time the animal picks up its front foot, its body and its hindfoot have moved some distance forward. The hindfoot is then put on the ground very close to where the forefoot was a moment earlier. Because of this, in trackways of quadrupedal dinosaurs, the hindfoot track is often very close behind the forefoot track of the same side of the body. If

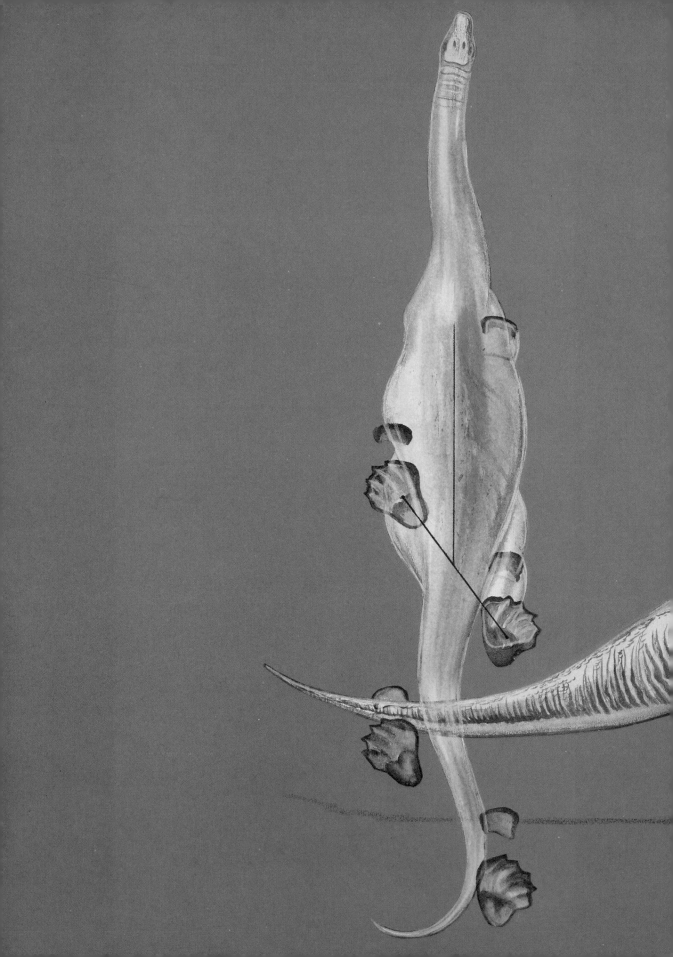

Walking quadrupedal dinosaurs, like these sauropods, often put their hindfeet on the ground close behind where their forefeet had been. Sometimes the distance from the dinosaur's shoulders to its hips can be estimated from the positions of the forefoot and hindfoot tracks. For the see-through sauropod, the shoulder-to-hip distance is the distance from the top right forefoot track to the middle of a line connecting two hindfoot tracks.

54

prints of both forefeet and hindfeet are preserved in the trackway, paleontologists can use the positions of these tracks to estimate the distance from the dinosaur's shoulders to its hips.

Sometimes, though, the dinosaur's weight on the hindfoot squeezed sediment forward to squash the forefoot track from the rear. Sometimes the hindfoot even came down right on top of the forefoot track, wiping it out.

Ornithopod dinosaurs may have switched back and forth between walking on two and four legs. Trackways thought to have been made by ornithopods changing from quadrupedal to bipedal walking show that when the dinosaur got off its front legs, the stride length and pace angulation of its hindfoot trackway increased. Ornithopods may have walked on four feet only when they were moving slowly, perhaps while they were feeding.

Early Cretaceous sauropod trackway from the Paluxy River, Dinosaur Valley State Park, Glen Rose, Texas. Tracks of the front feet are just in front of tracks of the hindfeet. The hindfoot tracks are about 77 centimeters long. Footprints like this are called *Brontopodus*, and were probably made by a sauropod called *Pleurocoelus.*

CHAPTER SEVEN

What Footprints Tell Us about Dinosaur Behavior

Paleontologists studying the bones of a dinosaur can discover much about how the living dinosaur behaved by finding out how it died, and how its skeleton was preserved as a fossil. If the dinosaur's bones were found along with other skeletons of the same kind of dinosaur, paleontologists might guess that this kind of dinosaur had lived in herds. But this might not be true. Large numbers of dinosaurs might have died in one place for other reasons. During a drought, for example, many dinosaurs that usually kept to themselves might have come to the last remaining pond in an area, and then died when it finally dried up, or when all the food in the area of the pond was gone.

Since finding many skeletons of the same kind of dinosaur in one place does not by itself always prove that those dinosaurs lived in herds, a paleontologist needs additional, different evidence to back up the large number of similar skeletons. Dinosaur trackways are just that kind of evidence.

Let us imagine the muddy shore of an ancient lake during the age of the dinosaurs. If dinosaurs and other animals walked by themselves at different times across this muddy surface, each animal would have been traveling in its own direction. Some animals might have moved into and out of the water, and other animals might have walked along the lakeshore. We would expect the footprints made by all of the different kinds of trackmakers to head in many directions.

If, however, the animals usually preferred to walk along the water's edge, we would expect some trails to be heading in one direction along the shore, and many trackways to be going in the opposite direction. This is, in fact, what is often seen when we find dinosaur trackways. Such a back-and-forth arrangement of trackways could have been made by groups of dinosaurs walking in both directions along the shoreline, but could just as well have been made by dinosaurs walking alone, one at a time.

Now suppose that most of the dinosaur trails showed the back-and-forth arrangement, but that all of the trackways of one of the kinds of dinosaur went in only one of the two directions. We might be able to think of reasons why dinosaurs of that one kind could have passed through the area at different times, all of them heading the same way. It might be easier to explain these trackways, however, if they had been made by a herd of animals moving through the area all at one time. There are, in fact, places where we see just this arrangement of dinosaur tracks.

One of these places is the bed of the Paluxy River, near the town of Glen Rose, Texas, in Dinosaur Valley State Park. In the rocks of the riverbed are many dinosaur footprints that were made during the early part of the Cretaceous Period. Most of these tracks were made by large carnivorous dinosaurs. They show the back-and-forth kind of arrangement already described.

In the same rocks, however, can be found even bigger footprints—some a meter or more in length—that were made by sauropod dinosaurs. Unlike the theropod trails, all of the sauropod trackways head in the same direction,

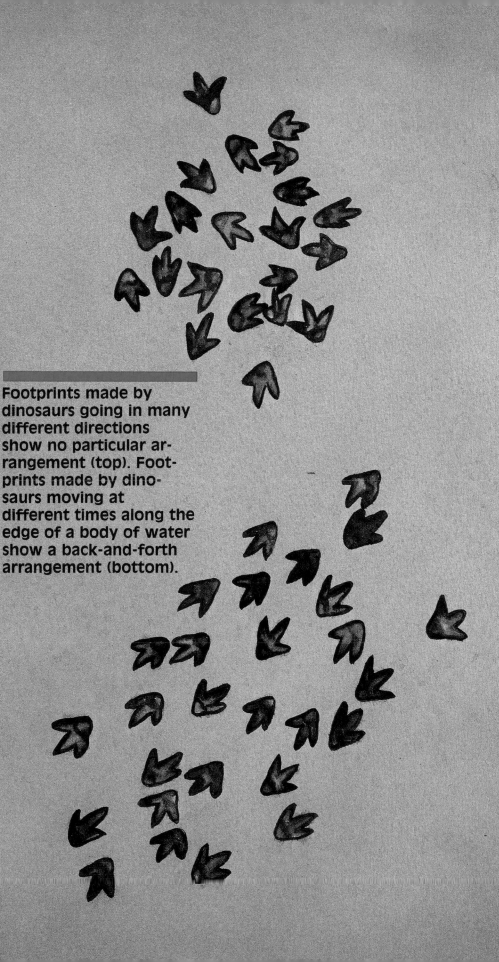

Footprints made by
dinosaurs going in many
different directions
show no particular ar-
rangement (top). Foot-
prints made by dino-
saurs moving at
different times along the
edge of a body of water
show a back-and-forth
arrangement (bottom).

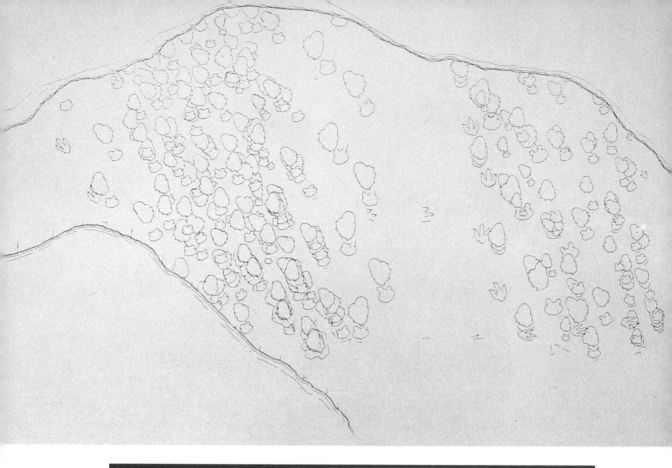

Trackways of Early Cretaceous sauropods from a site near Bandera, Texas. The largest footprints are about 70 centimeters long. Three-toed tracks of theropods also occur here.

suggesting that they were made by a herd of these huge reptiles.

Even more convincing evidence of a sauropod herd comes from Cretaceous rocks near Bandera, Texas. Here were found trails of about twenty-three sauropods, all of which were made by animals traveling in the same direction. Some of these trackways were made by sauropods much smaller than those of the Paluxy River. The Bandera herd had both young, small sauropods and older, larger sauropods. The bigger sauropods may have been the parents, or maybe the older brothers and sisters, of the smaller sauropod dinosaurs.

Trackway evidence of sauropod herds has also been found at places outside Texas. One of these is the Jurassic lakeshore in southeastern Colorado already described. The arrangement of the sauropod trackways at this place suggests not only that the dinosaurs were traveling in a herd, but perhaps also that smaller, younger sauropods were surrounded by bigger dinosaurs, possibly to protect them from carnivorous dinosaurs.

Possibly the most striking trackway evidence of herding in dinosaurs involves ornithopods. At about the same time as the Paluxy River and Bandera footprints were made, other dinosaurs were leaving footprints in British Columbia, in what is today the canyon of the Peace River. Huge three-toed prints of ornithopods and theropods are common in rocks of this area.

At one place, four ornithopod trackways are very close together, all heading in the same direction. The trails curve back and forth—some more than others—but do not cross each other. At one point, one of the trackways bends sharply to the left. The trail next to it also bends to the left, but not as sharply. The third and fourth trackways also bend to the left, but only slightly. Because all of the trails show the same shift, it is likely that the trackmakers were walking close together, side by side. When one of them shifted its position, the other dinosaurs had to do the same to avoid colliding with each other. The dinosaur closest to the animal that first changed its course had to move the most, and the dinosaurs further away only had to change their courses a little bit.

Trackways also provide evidence about the behavior of meat-eating dinosaurs. Alongside one of the Paluxy River sauropod trails was the trackway of a big theropod. In a few places the theropod stepped into, and partly squashed, the sauropod's tracks. Where the sauropod's

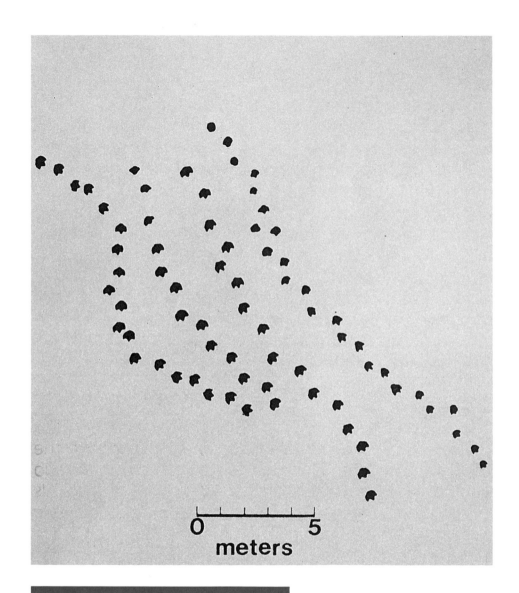

0 — meters — 5

Trackways of Early Cretaceous ornithopods from the Peace River Canyon, British Columbia, Canada

Trackways of a sauropod dinosaur and a theropod that was probably following the sauropod. Paluxy River, Dinosaur Valley State Park, Glen Rose, Texas

A large theropod dinosaur, *Acrocanthosaurus*, attacks a sauropod, *Pleurocoelus*, in this interpretation of how the Paluxy River dinosaur footprint site may have been made. A second theropod comes to join the attack as the rest of the sauropod herd flees. A small ornithopod runs away to the left, and two larger ornithopods in the background watch the fight, as pterosaurs fly overhead.

trail made a curve to the left, the theropod's trackway made the same bend. The theropod was probably following the sauropod, but we don't know if it finally attacked and killed it.

Some of the other sauropod trails in the Paluxy riverbed also had theropod trackways nearby. Could it be that the group of sauropods was followed by a pack of carnivorous dinosaurs? The evidence is not clear enough to say. However, at many other places around the world, trackways of meat-eating dinosaurs are sometimes found heading in the same direction. Some of these places may well record the existence of theropod packs.

We have seen how dinosaur footprints were made, and how they became fossils. We have learned that fossil trackways can show us how dinosaurs walked and ran, and whether they lived in groups.

However, there is still much that paleontologists do not understand about dinosaur footprints. We need to know more about the processes by which tracks were formed and fossilized. We need to learn if there are better ways to identify the dinosaurs that made the tracks we find. We want to be able to use dinosaur footprints as tools—along with dinosaur skeletons—in understanding when different kinds of dinosaurs lived in different parts of the world.

Dinosaur footprints continue to be found in great numbers and in many places, and paleontologists are constantly discovering new ways to study these trace fossils. For a long time to come, we will still be on the tracks of the dinosaurs.

Glossary

Bipedal—a word used to describe an animal that walks on two legs (its hind legs)

Body fossils—the fossilized shells, bones, or other body parts of ancient animals

Carnivore—a meat-eating animal

Coprolite—the fossilized droppings of an ancient animal

Eras—great lengths of time in earth history; eras containing several *periods* of geologic time

Erosion—process that loosens rocks or sediments and carries them away from the places where they formed

Extinct—no longer existing

Fauna—a list of the kinds of animals that lived in a certain place and time

Flightless birds—ground-living birds whose wings are too small and poorly developed to permit them to fly

Geologists—scientists who study the earth and its history

Ghost tracks (undertracks)—impressions formed in sediments below (sometimes above) the sediment layer on which a track-making animal actually walked

Herbivore—a plant-eating animal

Mineral—a naturally occurring solid that has an orderly arrangement of atoms and a definite chemical composition, causing it to have a given set of physical and chemical properties

Natural cast—a footprint filled by sediment; a footprint cast sticking out from the underside of the rock that formed from the sediment that covered the layer on which the trackmaker walked

Natural mold—an impression made by an animal's foot in the upper side of a sedimentary layer; in other words, an actual footprint

Ornithischian dinosaurs—dinosaurs that had a hip skeleton something like that of birds

Ornithopods—plant-eating *ornithischian dinosaurs* that walked part of the time on two legs and part of the time on four

Pace—the distance between a print of the right forefoot and the next left forefoot, or between the right hindfoot and the next left hindfoot, or from a left track to the next right track

Pace angulation—the angle formed by two successive paces

Paleontologists—scientists who study fossils

Periods—lengths of geologic time

Quadrupedal—a word that describes an animal that walks on all four legs

Saurischian dinosaurs—dinosaurs that had a hip skeleton similar to that of most other reptiles

Sauropods—herbivorous dinosaurs with a long neck and tail, small head, and five-toed limbs

Sediments—pieces of rock or other materials that pile up on the earth's surface

Stride—the distance between a left forefoot or hindfoot and the next left forefoot or hindfoot, or between two right forefeet or hindfeet

Theropods—meat-eating *saurischian dinosaurs*

Trace fossil—a footprint, burrow, nest, bite mark, *coprolite*, or any other record of the activities of an ancient animal

Trackway (trail)—a series of footprints made one after the other by the same animal

Trail—see *trackway*

Undertracks—see *ghost tracks*

Weathering—physical and chemical processes that work at or near the earth's surface and that change minerals or break rocks into sediments

For Further Reading

Allen, Tom, Jane D. Allen, and Savannah Waring Walker. *Dinosaur Days in Texas.* Dallas, Tex.: Hendrick-Long Publishing, 1989.

Benton, Michael. *The Dinosaur Encyclopedia.* New York: Wanderer Books, 1984.

Bird, Roland T. *Bones for Barnum Brown: Adventures of a Dinosaur Hunter.* Fort Worth: Texas Christian University Press, 1985.

Glut, Donald F. *The New Dinosaur Dictionary.* Secaucus, N.J.: Citadel Press, 1982.

Horner, John R., and James Gorman. *Digging Dinosaurs.* New York: Workman Publishing, 1988.

Lambert, David. *A Field Guide to Dinosaurs.* New York: Avon Books, 1983.

National Wildlife Federation. *Ranger Rick's Dinosaur Book.* Washington, D.C.: National Wildlife Federation, 1984.

Norman, David. *When Dinosaurs Ruled the Earth.* New York: Exeter Books, 1985.

Wexo, John Bonnett. *Dinosaurs.* Mankato, Minn.: Creative Education, 1989.

About the Author

James O. Farlow has a Ph.D. in geology from Yale University. He is a professor of geology at Indiana University–Purdue University at Fort Wayne. Dr. Farlow has written many scientific and popular articles about dinosaurs and their footprints.

About the Illustrator

Doris Tischler of Austin, Texas, is a nationally known artist for the natural sciences. She has not only illustrated several books and National Park Service exhibits but has also prepared major museum paleontological exhibits in Texas, Utah, New Mexico, Virginia, and Canada.

70

Index